PROFIT MAXIMIZATION

The Ethical Mandate of Business

T0130874

Patrick Primeaux and John Stieber

PROFIT MAXIMIZATION

The Ethical Mandate of Business

Patrick Primeaux and John Stieber

Austin & Winfield
San Francisco - London - Bethesda
1995

Library of Congress Cataloging-in-Publication Data

Primeaux, Patrick.
    Profit maximization : the ethical mandate of business / Patrick
Primeaux and John Stieber.
       p. cm.
    Includes bibliographical references and index.
    ISBN 1-57292-025-4 (cloth : alk. paper). -- ISBN 1-57292-024-6 (pbk.:
alk. paper).
    1. Business ethics. 2. Profit--Moral and ethical aspects. I. Stieber,
John. II. Title.
HF5387.P737 1995
174'.4--dc20   95-49232
                                            CIP

Copyright 1995 by Patrick Primeaux

Editorial Inquiries:
Austin & Winfield, Publishers
7831 Woodmont Avenue, #345
Bethesda, MD 20814
(301) 654-7335

To Order: (800) 99-AUSTIN

To Fran, Ginger, and Jack Jr.

Contents

Introduction

There is an ancient Greek saying that a big book is a bad book. It is a saying to which more academics should pay more attention. On the grounds of length, the ancient Greeks would have been pleased with this book. The authors come straight to their points, with proper attention to clarifications, justifications and examples. Businesspeople interested in a brief introduction to business ethics should find this book an attractive beginning.

As Editor-in-Chief of the *Journal of Business Ethics* since its first issue in 1980, I have had one main disappointment. That is that relatively few practitioners subscribe to and read the *Journal*. Because it is primarily a scholarly journal, my co-editor, Deborah Poff and I always expected it would be a vehicle of communication primarily for scholars. But we hoped and still hope that we could attract practitioners, people in business full-time, into the discussions. Alas, very few have taken the bait, and I suspect that one of the main reasons is the language of the academy.

A good scholar, it has been said, writes for eternity. Unfortunately, the remark is ambiguous but true in at least two senses. The good sense of the remark is that good ideas and good literature do stand the test of time. The bad sense of the remark is that good scholars seem to take forever to say what they have to say. Again, this is not a problem for the authors of this book, and that means that I think this book will provide a bridge between the academy and businesspeople that is much to be desired.

I also think that the substantive argument of the book will be attractive to practicing businesspeople. The basic position of the authors is pragmatic. In their own words: "What we have tried to demonstrate is that the behavior of profit maximization includes an examination of the opportunity costs associated with all business decisions, and that ethical considerations represent some, although not all, of the opportunity costs of a given decision. ...Profit maximization discourages flagrant disregard for community standards of pollution, safety, exploitation of human and natural resources, etc. ...In fact, issues raised by philosophical, religious, and legal concerns are also concerns of business and its required sensitivity to the community as embodied in opportunity costs."

It would be remarkable if a book on business ethics pleased everyone who might have an interest in the topic. Although I like the authors' pragmatic approach to business ethics and especially their insistence upon a very robust analysis of benefits and costs going beyond mere dollars and cents, there are many things we would have to negotiate in order to reach concensus. Fortunately for us, the authors and I work in a profession that allows us the luxury of being able to carry out precisely such negotiations. Fortunately for other people, they will be able to consider the authors' treatise without listening to our negotiations.

--Alex C. Michalos

Foreword

During an interview with the Chairman and CEO of a Fortune 500 company, we asked whether he would consider a seminar in business ethics for his company. His response was immediate and negative: any discussion of business ethics would send a signal to his stockholders that the company was unethical, and his managers and employees that they were unethical.

We weren't at all surprised by his defensive posture. Why? Partly because "business ethics" has become associated with abuse and mismanagement. Partly because "business ethics" is a relatively new term, a misunderstood concept, that frightens managers. And, partly because men and women in business do not understand business ethics as central and integral to the business enterprise, even though they usually behave as though it is.

The problem is twofold. First, what business people hear and read about business ethics comes from outsiders: philosophical, religious, and legal theorists. What these theorists know is good and valid, but limited. Their arguments are valid only within their own spheres of thought, only within their own self-imposed boundaries. To argue and defend their assumptions they become detractors of our economic system and of men and women in business. Consequently, they universalize exceptions and characterize men and women in business as seeking money and power for its own sake.

It is no secret that theorists assess practitioners negatively. Theorists theorize. That is what they do best, but so often theorists lose the forest for the trees, and when assessing business from a philosophical, theological, or legal perspective, lose sight of the basic fact that business is much more practical than theoretical.

The other side of the problem is that the men and women in business are so consumed by the practical aspects of their work, that they do not step back to identify and assess their goals or the means of accomplishing those goals. They find it increasingly difficult to articulate their real ethics and the means to realize them. They also find it difficult to articulate their business ethics, even though, for the most part, they are already pursuing good business ethics.

That articulation cannot originate in philosophy, religion, or law. In fact, we categorically reject the notion that philosophy, religion, or law can identify the business enterprise and business ethics for business. That identification can arise only in business itself.

Today, perhaps more than ever, it has become a matter of urgency for business to retrieve its own ethics from philosophical, religious, and legal theorists. This little book attempts to do just that.

We assume a positive and optimistic view of business and of the men and women in business. The role of business has always been, and continues to be, that of enriching society by providing goods and services people need and want. Men and women in business want to do the right thing, and they want to pursue good ethics for themselves and for society as a whole. They know that good ethics is good business.

Patrick Primeaux
St. John's University, New York

John A. Stieber
Southern Methodist University, Dallas

I

The

Paradigm

of

Profit

Maximization

Business is the highest level of human activity and the highest level of social good.

We believe that some of the greatest pieces of art the world has ever known are a good meal, a Boeing 747, a BMW, a personal computer, a CAT scanner, a refrigerator.

By any measure, the kind of behavior needed to produce these works of art constitutes the highest level of human activity and the highest level of social good. After all, it is people engaged in business who deliver all of the goods and services the community wants, such as better health care, schools for our children, food for our tables, and shelter for our families.

Business demands excellence and creativity. Men and women in business are artists and scientists. The activities in which they engage are like those required to produce a great symphony, a well-written play, a fine painting, a vintage wine, a piece of sculptured glass, or a new scientific discovery. These activities demand excellence and require an abundance of creativity.

We've just used two powerful words to describe human achievement: excellence and creativity. For men and women in business, these two words translate directly into efficiency. By efficiency we mean the best use of scarce resources.

Remember the story of Adam and Eve? When they were inside the Garden of Eden, they had everything they wanted. Why? They had an infinite number of resources available to them. When they found themselves outside the Garden, they found themselves with a limited number of resources. Moreover, they found that to acquire the things they wanted, they had to use these scarce resources efficiently.

The Paradigm of Profit Maximization

The primary objective of any human enterprise, but especially that of business, is to use scarce resources efficiently. In fact, the success or failure of any business person is measured by the amount of goods and services produced from a given set of scarce resources. Those who produce the most are efficient; those who produce less are inefficient.

The human behavior driving this efficiency is described in the paradigm of profit maximization. When business men and women profit maximize, i.e., allocate resources efficiently, people have more of the things they want, and that is good. When they do not profit maximize, i.e., allocate scarce resources inefficiently, people have less of the things they want, and that is bad.

The Paradigm of Profit Maximization

Since ethics is basically a study of good and bad activity, the decision to profit maximize or not to profit maximize becomes a question of applied or practical ethics.

This is especially true if the things they want are food, health care, education, and the other necessities of life.

All business people have an ethical mandate to profit maximize. Throughout this book, whenever we equate efficiency and good ethics, we assume human limitation and imply that men and women want to maximize their own potential as well as that of the business--within human limitations. The opposite would also hold. The person failing to maximize his or her own potential and that of the business would be considered inefficient and, consequently, unethical.

Since profit maximization describes the behavior that results in the efficient allocation of resources, the question of whether or not to maximize profits is an ethical question. Therefore, all business people have an ethical mandate to profit maximize.

The Paradigm of Profit Maximization

We have tied excellence and creativity to efficiency, and efficiency to profit maximization, and profit maximization to ethics.

Most men and women in business think of profit maximization as maximizing the bottom line. Essentially, this is an accounting perspective, and it is not an unexpected interpretation. However, that is not what we mean by profit maximization.

On the other hand, men and women who do think that maximizing bottom-line profits, and only that, constitutes good business are really not business people at all. Call them what you will--greedy promoters, self-aggrandizing opportunists, criminals--but don't call them business people. They have no place in the discussion of business activity or business ethics.

Obviously, any business person, physician, plumber, airline pilot, lawyer, educator, clergyman, etc. who uses his or her profession for purely selfish gain does so in violation of one's profession.

What exactly is profit maximization? Rather than concentrating on the bottom line, profit maximization focuses on the behavior that leads directly into bottom line profits or losses. Rather than concentrating on numbers, profit maximization focuses on all of those human activities that produce those numbers.

When we use the phrase "Paradigm of Profit Maximization" we are referring to everything and anything that goes into good business. That is, the "Paradigm of Profit Maximization" refers to everything that goes into converting scarce resources into what people want.

From a technical perspective, profit maximization is defined as the set of conditions where marginal revenue is equal to marginal cost (MR=MC), and where the marginal cost curve intersects the marginal revenue curve from below. It is at that point, and only at that point, that a firm operates at a level of efficiency that guarantees the community of consumers the maximum amount of goods and services produced from a given set of scarce resources.

These efficiencies are usually calculated mathematically, and rarely translated into behavioral expectations. Our discussion moves from the more abstract mathematics to the more practical behavior, and concentrates on the ethical implications common to both.

The Paradigm of Profit Maximization

We define profit maximization in behavioral terms:

Producing the right kind and the right amount of goods and services the consumer wants at the lowest possible cost.

Who determines "the right kind"? Basically, it is the market place. Businesses know they are producing the right kind of goods and services if there is a market demand for them, i.e., if consumers are willing to pay a price for them.

Decidedly, the market relies on individual judgment and decision-making. On the one hand, it is an individual who determines what to purchase or not to purchase. On the other hand, it is an individual who determines what to produce or not to produce. Determination or judgment implies ethical considerations, as does the phrase "the right kind."

The Paradigm of Profit Maximization

Ethical considerations about the purchase or production of goods and services will be determined and/or regulated by the market in compliance with the free choice of individuals.

Who determines whether consumers want to smoke cigarettes or drink diet colas? The individual consumers do! Were individual consumers to judge that they did not want these products, they would not be produced. If the producer judged, in conscience, that he or she should not produce these items, they would not be produced--at least not by this producer. They could, however, be produced by another whose ethics would allow him or her to do so.

There is another way to determine what consumers purchase: *lobbying* and *boycotting*. For whatever reason or motivation, people can (and do) organize to advocate the creation of a new product or the elimination of an already-existing one.

The motivation directing these groups is never that of profit maximization. It arises outside of business, and is often religious, legal, or philosophical in origin.

That is not to pretend that these advocacy groups have no influence on business or profit maximization. It is, rather, to identify the origins of these movements outside of profit maximization and, as we are arguing, to situate their influences in opportunity costs.

The Paradigm of Profit Maximization

Assume you make cars. You produce a car and take it to the marketplace. As long as the price people are willing to pay for that car is greater than the cost of producing it, you will sell it. In the technical jargon of profit maximization, one would say that you would bring the car to market as long as the marginal revenue from the sale of the car is greater than the marginal cost of producing the car.

You will continue to bring additional cars to the market as long as the price for each of these cars is greater than the cost of producing each additional car. In fact, you will continue to do so until that point where the price of the car begins to approach the cost; or, to the point where marginal revenue from the sale of the car is equal to the marginal cost of producing the car.

Once your marginal cost begins to exceed your marginal revenue, you will no longer bring cars to the marketplace because you will lose money on these units.

The Paradigm of Profit Maximization

Many think of profit as a return on investment. Interest in the form of dividends and increased stock value is the return on investment. Profit is the reward for creativity and excellence, for efficiency or profit maximizing behavior, and for good business and good business ethics.

Certainly, you're not going to bring the car to the market if the cost to produce it is greater than the price people are willing to pay for it, i.e., if marginal revenue is less than marginal cost. It would be inefficient to sell things for less than they cost. You would incur losses. It would also be unethical because it is inefficient. You, the producer, as well as the consumer, would lose because you are not allocating resources efficiently.

What are goods and services? We ordinarily think in terms of cars, computers, televisions, clothes, theater, sports, maintenance, utilities. In short, goods and services are anything consumers want and are willing to pay for. Even ethics falls under this definition.

We've been using the word "wants" as a verb without any kind of qualification or distinction. We have done so deliberately to call attention to the fact that the individual consumers judge or determine for themselves the kind and the amount of goods and services they wish to purchase.

Often the word "needs" rather than the word "wants" is used in this kind of discussion. "Needs" implies value judgments that are imposed by others on the individual consumers. To a certain point that is inevitable: everyone needs food, water, oxygen, health care, clothing, shelter. But, even then, what the consumer wants goes beyond what he or she needs. The word "wants" refers to all of the conceivable things the individual would like to have, including needs.

Producing at the lowest possible cost is probably the most recognizable concern of business men and women. The costs of production for any firm can be, and usually are, divided into two basic categories: *fixed costs* and *variable costs*

Fixed costs are those costs of production that remain constant. For a farmer, his land would be a fixed cost.

Variable costs are those costs of production that change. For a greater yield of corn, our farmer will buy more seed, more fertilizer, and hire more harvesters.

The Paradigm of Profit Maximization

For the farmer the ethical implications of fixed and variable costs are obvious. He has to bring in enough income to cover them. Should he fail to do so because of his own inefficiencies, he is failing to profit maximize, and is unethical.

When our farmer is careless and wastes fertilizer, his costs rise which means he is not producing at the lowest possible cost. Is he being inefficient? Yes. Is he being unethical? Yes. Is he maximizing profits? No.

II
Profit
Maximization
and
Opportunity
Costs

When men and women in business analyze the reasons for the farmer's higher costs, they do so in terms of inefficiencies. These inefficiencies are usually addressed in reference to opportunity costs.

24

Opportunity costs are those goods and services that
will not be produced from a given set of scarce
resources because these same resources were used to
produce something else. Once our farmer uses his
land to produce corn in a given crop year, he cannot
grow wheat on that same land. His opportunity costs
are the wheat that could have been produced on the
land, but was not produced.

Within the broad perspective of an infinite number
of opportunity costs, we can distinguish two basic
kinds: 1) those tied to internal inefficiencies in
decision-making; and 2) those tied to external
conditions.

Another way to distinguish the two would be in terms of those concerns over which managers can be expected to exercise responsibility and control, and, simply stated, those over which managers cannot be expected to exercise responsibility and control.

We can expect our farmer to exercise good land management, rotating crops, replenishing vital nutrients, etc. If he fails to do so, his opportunity costs are the lost revenues from crop yield reductions. These opportunity costs to himself (and higher food costs to others) are matters of inefficiency and poor business ethics. The ethical consideration here, as well as the profit maximization consideration, is that he has an obligation to maintain the quality of his land--a scarce resource.

Should the farmer suffer crop yield reductions because of unexpected and unpredictable drought, flooding, and hurricanes, there is nothing he can do. These opportunity costs exist and are incurred by the farmer, but he cannot be accused of inefficient land management or unethical behavior.

However, profit maximization would demand that the farmer try to insure against these externalities. To ignore them would involve opportunity costs.

We are arguing that the ethical mandate for business itself, and for business men and women, is profit maximization. We mentioned earlier that profit maximization focuses on the behavior that leads directly into bottom line profits and losses. Our primary focus, then, is not bottom line profit or loss, but the human behavior that the bottom-line numbers reflect.

The behavior of profit maximization, as it relates to the bottom line, will guarantee one of two things: that if you have profits, they will be maximized; that if you have losses, they will be minimized. Therefore, the argument that profit maximization refers to maximizing the bottom line regardless of how it is done, and without considering its consequences, has no validity and should be dismissed. Unfortunately, it is not.

Profit Maximization and Opportunity Costs

Earlier we concentrated on profit maximizing behavior in terms of converting scarce resources into goods and services. Scarce resources can be grouped into four basic components: *land, labor-time, capital, creativity/entrepreneurship.* It is the unethical behavior directly related to the use of each of these scarce resources that results in opportunity costs. The unethical behavior to which we are referring is the inefficient use of these resources.

When referring to the use of scarce resources, it is important to recognize what kind of payments are made to bring these resources into the productive process. The payment to land is *rent*. The payment to capital is *interest* (dividends and increased stock values). The payment to labor-time is *wages*. The payment to creativity/entrepreneurship is *profit*.

Profit Maximization and Opportunity Costs

Ordinarily, profit is considered payment to stockholders, who own the capital, rather than to creativity. Properly speaking, the payment to stockholders is not profit, but interest. Profit accrues from creativity/entrepreneurship, and it is the creative individuals within a given firm who generate profit. Failure to distribute profit to these creative people is one of the greatest opportunity costs that firms incur, and they are usually oblivious to these costs. The reason that firms incur these opportunity costs is that creative people leave, often to create their own firms. Any time a firm loses a creative person (because they are not paid for their creativity), that firm is behaving inefficiently, and, consequently, unethically. Why?

Someone else would have to be hired. The company would incur hiring costs which could have been avoided by paying the original employee for his or her creative contribution. The hiring costs that could have been avoided, and the loss of the creativity of the person who left, are the opportunity costs for the firm. These are scarce resources that could have been put to better use.

Profit Maximization and Opportunity Costs

32

Defining profit as payment to creativity/ entrepreneurship is not as radical and disruptive a recommendation as it first seems. Thinking of shareholders and/or owners receiving interest from their investment would imply fixed, limited return on investment and would seriously impede investment.

However, this does not mean that owners and investors would be excluded from the profit designated as payment to creativity/ entrepreneurship. Investors, as well as managers and employees, along with all of the stakeholders with an interest in, or affected by, the business, could participate in this profit-sharing. The basic mandate is that profit be defined as payment to creativity/entrepreneurship, and awarded to individuals in direct proportion to their contribution to revenues.

The investors who takes a creative risk in providing capital for a new company or product, the director who recommends a successful diversification strategy, the manager who initiates an effective advertising campaign, the janitor who discovers a more efficient cleaning agent--all contribute to efficiency and to revenues, and should be rewarded for their creativity/entrepreneurship.

Profit Maximization and Opportunity Costs

The object of business is not simply that of enhancing or maximizing shareholders' investment. The object of business, according to the principles of profit maximization, is to enhance everyone's personal investment in the business, and to reward that investment in proportion to one's contribution to its revenues. This is what leads to the maximization of the shareholders' investment. This is the only way to maximize the shareholders' investment.

There is, then, an underlying ethical mandate belonging to everyone exercising responsibility for the business, to maximize his or her own potential share of the profit. Realizing the kinds of inter-relational and cooperative dynamics implied in this common objective, profit maximization is not a mandate for individual self-aggrandizement or personal greed. It is, by its very definition, a communal and social mandate.

Profit Maximization and Opportunity Costs

We have already shown how poor land management generated opportunity costs for the farmer. His decision to mismanage his land resource was inefficient, unethical, and resulted in opportunity costs.

The basic, underlying principle for land management is to ensure its highest-valued use. In Plano, Texas, the corporate offices of Frito Lay are located on a piece of land that not only holds its buildings, but is beautifully landscaped to create an environment that is attractive to its employees and the community in which it resides. Frito Lay obviously determined that an attractive environmental setting would encourage its employees to be more productive.

The prospect of future increases in the size of the buildings raises a question of ethics and opportunity costs. What is the highest valued use of that land? Clearly, that piece of land is a scarce resource. Is the use of the land more valuable to Frito Lay and its mandate to profit maximize in its present form? Or, is the use of the land more valuable with less environmental quality and more office space?

Stated another way, does the increased productivity from additional office space offset the possible decrease in employee productivity resulting from a lower quality environment? To choose the less valuable use of the land would be inefficient and unethical. Clearly, there would be opportunity costs resulting from the wrong decision.

Profit Maximization and Opportunity Costs

When Robinson Crusoe was first stranded on a deserted island, he found himself spending all of his time gathering food. A large part of his diet was shellfish. He had a difficult time opening clam shells. One day, he decided to do something about it, and created a piece of capital. He took a stone, a stick, a raw hemp and made a hammer.

What does Robinson Crusoe's new hammer tell us about profit maximization, efficiency, and ethical behavior? While gathering food in his less inventive days, Robinson Crusoe was as efficient as he could have been at that time. Hence, his business behavior was ethical. Once he thought about making the hammer, which would increase his efficiency in food gathering, the only correct ethical decision he could make was to proceed with making the hammer. As the story goes, that hammer (a piece of capital) freed up his time to do other things.

These "other things" would be the opportunity costs of not making the hammer. Many individuals and companies have recently discovered the need to make the same kind of decision with regard to personal computers. If those computers were to improve their productivity, it would have been unethical not to purchase them (assuming they had the means to pay for them). Why? Because the computers enable them to do more of the same things in a given period of time, thereby providing additional goods and services. The opportunity costs of not acquiring the computers are that those additional goods and services would never have been realized. On the other hand, there is also the possibility of waste, i.e., buying a computer which impedes rather than enhances productivity, or buying a computer which provides technology surpassing the needs of the company.

Profit Maximization and Opportunity Costs

In a labor climate demanding ever higher labor skills, it is becoming more difficult to establish wage rates consistent with the increased productivities they represent. When a skilled employee is paid insufficient wages relative to what he or she can command in the marketplace, there is a good chance that employee will move on.

Someone else would have to be hired; and at market wage. The company would incur hiring costs which could have been avoided by paying the original employee the same market wage paid the new employee. The hiring costs, that could have been avoided, are the opportunity costs of the firm. These resources could have been used for something else. The company would be unethical, failing to maximize profits by not paying the original employee his or her market wage.

We have already discussed opportunity costs and creativity/entrepreneurship with respect to profits as payment to this scarce resource. Since it is creative individuals who generate profit for the firm, if they do not share in that profit, the firm is being inefficient, unethical, and failing to profit-maximize. These creative people will leave. The profit of the firm will decline. This lost profit is the opportunity cost the firm will incur by failing to pay its valuable, scarce, creative human resources.

Profit Maximization and Opportunity Costs

One specialized resource we've left out of this discussion of opportunity costs is the decision-making manager who is sensitive to, and aware of, the *ethos* and *mores* of the total human community.

Managers are usually described as those who are concerned with the internal allocation of scarce resources, and the conversion of these resources into goods and services. The manager we're interested in is the one who looks beyond these internal dynamics, and is aware of external concerns which directly and indirectly impact profits. This is the manager who is so attuned to the intricate relationship between these internal dynamics and external concerns that he or she beings all of these considerations into the profit-maximizing decisions of the firm.

In fact, profit maximization demands this kind of manager. Any other kind of manager will be inefficient, unethical, and incur opportunity costs for the firm.

Profit Maximization and Opportunity Costs

There are two key phrases in our definition of opportunity costs that warrant further attention. These two phrases are: "the goods and services that will not be produced" and "from a given set of resources."

Suppose a firm has a fixed amount of money from the earnings it has retained to invest for its owners. These retained earnings can be used to buy scarce resources, and are being retained for future use, e.g., expansion, more efficient technology, etc. The firm then decides to build a barbecue pork sandwich shop in the Moslem sector of a city.

Once these resources ("a given set of resources") are committed to the project, they can never be used to produce any other goods and services for the community, such as health care, education, or housing ("the goods and services that will be produced").

Besides the usual business considerations required of this decision (location, lease costs, food costs, hiring, taxes, etc.), there is a serious ethical consideration that must be addressed. Moslems do not eat pork. Were managers insensitive to this ethical behavior, the project would fail.

If the project fails (as it is sure to do) it would be because the managers of this firm were insensitive to the ethics of the situation. They did not realize the significance of the ethical/moral beliefs of the dominant religion of the area. *For the community,* the opportunity costs would be that a whole set of scarce resources was wasted to produce something no one wanted. These scarce resources could never be used to produce something that the community wanted. *For the firm,* the opportunity costs would be that it will lose money from a set of scarce resources that could have been used to make money in another project.

From a broader perspective, what we see in this example is how managers who do not examine the *ethos* and *mores* of the community create negative economic consequences which represent opportunity costs for the business and for the community at large. These managers would not be profit maximizing precisely because they fail to consider the opportunity costs associated with the traditions, the customs, and the religious beliefs and practices of the community.

Any and every decision-making situation demands attention to external concerns which directly and indirectly impact profits. It is simply not enough to analyze the internal allocation and conversion of scarce resources into goods and services. The efficient manager considers both, and is, for this very reason, profit maximizing. To do otherwise would be inefficient and unethical.

Profit Maximization and Opportunity Costs

Usually the ethical considerations associated with a business decision are more complex than trying to sell barbecue pork in a Moslem community. In addition to the religious considerations, there is also a legal dimension to opportunity costs.

In November of 1976, a customer of General Motors took his 1977 Oldsmobile Delta '88 to a mechanic for servicing. The mechanic discovered a Chevrolet engine under the hood. The press picked up the story, and a flood of adverse publicity led to a storm of indignation. There were charges of fraud and unethical behavior as well as threats of individual class-action suits. In its defense, General Motors claimed it did no wrong, that interchanging parts was a common practice in the industry. The automobile manufacturer tried to explain the practice and demonstrated that its behavior was in the best interest of the consumer because it reduced costs. Five months later, in an attempt to stop public controversy and reduce its legal liability, General Motors offered a settlement to the affected car buyers.

Profit Maximization and Opportunity Costs

It has been estimated that the settlement was $40,000,000. There were also extensive legal costs which, to our knowledge, have never been revealed. These were dollars that could never be used again to develop or produce other goods and services.

There were, to be sure, other opportunity costs. We can surmise that a huge amount of human resource hours and energy were lost. Rather than directing these hours and energies to enhance the interests of stockholders, employees, and customers, they were used to put out fires and, of course, no one knows how many customers were

driven off or what it might cost to bring them back. More opportunity costs for the firm!

But, what if management did follow the prescribed behavior of profit maximization, and did conclude that its choice to interchange engines was consistent with the law? The problem is that legal considerations do not represent the whole spectrum of considerations required of opportunity-cost decision making.

Profit Maximization and Opportunity Costs

The difference between examining the ethical considerations of a decision and not examining them is absolutely crucial. No one expects men and women in business to be omnipotent. We can, however, expect them to consider ethical *mores* as they would any other opportunity costs when making decisions. If they do that, they are profit-maximizing. Sometimes, we forget that the nature of decision making is such that men and women, in good faith, can examine all of the available data and still make the wrong decision. *Good ethics does not guarantee perfection and good business ethics does not guarantee perfect decisions.*

Yet, are we to be content with minimalism, whether in theory or in practice? Surely someone in General Motors' management would have been aware that some potential buyers of Oldsmobiles would be unhappy with a Chevrolet engine. Even if it were a question of industry practice or industry standards to interchange automobile parts, would not the manager sensitive to that feeling among consumers be able to address the matter in such a way as to lead the company towards alternative action? Could that industry standard be turned into a competitive advantage of good will for their present and potential customers by declaring the substitution of engines? Or, could General Motors consider the long-term advantages of discontinuing the industry practice and turning it into another competitive advantage of good will by declaring its having done so?

Profit Maximization and Opportunity Costs

The firms that anticipated equal-opportunity legislation, by hiring minorities and women, and/or issuing guidelines against sexual harassment, have saved a great deal of money in opportunity costs. Those responding to the winds of change in business, and obviously not content with minimalism, will always benefit in the form of reduced opportunity costs.

Those that continue to adhere to minimal legal requirements will, in the long run, lose money as they try to catch up with those who anticipate and implement changes in social and cultural expectations.

In addition to the religious and legal aspects of opportunity costs, there are philosophical considerations. We are using "philosophy" here to portray a whole area of thinking and acting which is so basic to people that it is often taken for granted. Philosophical speculation has always advanced personal dignity and quality of life.

In the past fifty years or so that philosophical principle has taken on greater meaning for society in general, and for business in particular. Business has discovered over this period of time that many of its employees (scarce human resources) have personal difficulties that interfere with their performance at work. The sensitive employer has learned that failure to provide for remedies to these difficulties results in an opportunity cost for the firm in terms of lower productivity.

Profit Maximization and Opportunity Costs

III

Philosophy,

Religion,

and

Law

We have been situating business ethics in
opportunity costs. This understanding of business
ethics is useful because it 1) is grounded in business
theory and practice; 2) uses the language of business;
3) relates directly to the ordinary behavior of men
and women in business; and 4) is embodied in profit
maximization.

Profit maximization is a complete model, containing within itself all of the necessary assumptions and prescriptions required of business ethics. In effect, it provides a valid basis for ethical decision-making in business. It does so precisely by identifying the costs of doing business with the ethical implications of those costs. Our model also deals with these costs internally and externally. That is, it directs our attention to the internal costs of producing goods and services and also to the external costs associated with the greater society within which and for whom these goods and services are being produced. In other words, it is inefficient and unethical to consider the costs of production without, at the same time, considering the costs of social and cultural sensibilities.

Our model for business ethics also identifies a certain kind of manager as a specialized resource. That manager, as we explained earlier, is the person attuned to both the internal and external demands of profit-maximization. That manager will be aware of the costs of producing a certain chemical, and also aware of the costs of environmental pollution.

The basis for this awareness will not be some personal commitment to clean air, but a personal commitment to profit-maximization.

That commitment to profit-maximization is absolutely necessary for decision-making in business situations because it provides a common frame of reference. That is, it provides a common context wherein everyone speaks the same language and understands the implications of that language.

Moreover, it identifies business concerns directly with ethical concerns. There is, then, no need to focus one's attention outside of business to identify good business ethics.

There are many who would turn to academic philosophy for models for business ethics. Doing so would only create problems for men and women in business. It would require learning a totally new language and categories of thought. It would also require an energy-consuming application of that language and thought to business situations. That process would be, in our opinion, an inefficient use of time and energy.

Academic philosophy is, by its very nature, theoretical and speculative. It is removed from the practicalities of doing business, and consequently has little to offer the business men and women whose decisions are more practical and technical than speculative.

61

There is a growing tendency to speak of, and identify, business ethics with the law. Again, we can readily see that the objectives of the law and business differ. The biggest problem of equating business ethics with the law is that the law tends towards minimalism. It seeks a common denominator which is often addressed in terms of minimal restrictions. From that perspective, it is also negative, emphasizing what cannot be done. Business ethics, as we have presented here, is much more positive, emphasizing what needs to be done.

The law, although directed towards objectivity, is also subjective both in terms of origin and execution. Lawmakers are committed to their constituents and often influenced by special-interest lobbying groups. Jury decisions are also influenced and determined by persuasive arguments on the part of attorneys.

Rather than turning to academic philosophy or the law for business ethics, some are turning to religion. The basic question here is which religion. Or, to be even more precise, whose interpretation of a certain religious tradition? Within one's own country or within the expanding global market, we can no longer presume a common religious commitment or adherence to a common religious moral code.

Why, then, are men and women in business turning to academic philosophy, law, and religion for business ethics? It can be argued that these are the traditional voices for ethics in Western and American society. But, it can also be argued that they have little to offer business especially during this final decade of the twentieth century.

To be sure, philosophy, law, and religion are valid within their own assumptions and objectives. However, the assumptions and objectives of business are not those of philosophy, or of law, or of religion. On that basis alone, it would be invalid to superimpose onto business any assumptions and objectives than those of business itself, i.e., of profit-maximization. Likewise, it would be invalid to superimpose onto business any ethical model other than that of profit-maximization.

Philosophy, Religion, and Law

There is another problem involved in trying to superimpose philosophical, legal, or religious ethics onto business. They have not been able, even within their own theoretical assumptions, to resolve the problem of the one and the many, the individual and society, the relativist and the universalist. Which comes first, the individual or the group?

This problem has been resolved by business, somewhat in theory, but decidedly in practice. It is unthinkable that any individual involved in business would not be conscious and aware of others. It is of the very nature of business to provide goods and services to others. The dynamics of doing business, at its very heart and center, involves relationships.

Of course, men and women in business do not always step back to analyze the dynamics of these relationships or to theorize about their kind and quality. However, relationships do exist in the ordinary practice of conducting business, and in such a manner as to actually resolve the theoretical problems of individuality and commonality. No one can conduct business in isolation. Nor can anyone conduct business from a purely universalist or relativist perspective.

Given this rational quality of business, we can conclude that business not only stands alongside philosophy, religion, and law, as a valid enterprise, but in some ways surpasses them.

Philosophy, Religion, and Law

Accordingly, we can claim that in some ways, especially in its focus on the practical dimension of life, business can contribute to philosophy, religion, and law. The starting point of business theory is not some speculative principle, but the actual practice of business: men and women buying and selling in the marketplace. It enlists centuries of observing what works and what fails.

Perhaps the biggest difficulty for business with respect to philosophy, law, and religion is that men and women in business do not appreciate business as an enterprise valid within its own assumptions. They lack courage and self-confidence in their own work, feeling a need to defend that work by referring to philosophical, legal, or religious principles.

Perhaps, too, they do not appreciate the principles and assumptions of business. If they do not understand the need to be sensitive to costs of production, they will not be sensitive to the ethics inherent in the behavior associated with those costs.

Philosophy, Religion, and Law

We are not suggesting that academic philosophy, law, and religion do not affect the business enterprise. What we are recommending is that academic philosophy, law, and religion do not and cannot identify the business enterprise. Nor can they identify business ethics. Business is *sui generis*. It has a life of its own apart from any other practice or theory. And, on the most basic level of thought and behavior, it has an ethics of its own.

How do academic philosophy, law and religion affect business? They do so precisely with respect to opportunity costs. Philosophical, legal, and religious considerations belong to the *ethos* and *mores* of the greater society, of the world in which and for which business is pursued. To ignore, deny, or be insensitive to their existence is unethical for business because doing so will lead to higher costs and lower profits. That, as we have been arguing, is both inefficient and unethical.

We do consider philosophy, law, and religion within the profit-maximizing model. We do not, however, judge the profit-maximizing model according to their principles and mandates. Nor do we address business ethics primarily in terms of their assumptions and proscriptions.

Within their own assumptions, philosophy, law, and religion are valid as are the ethics arising from those assumptions. And, in ways too numerous to list, they have a direct bearing on the way individuals think and behave.

The final and ultimate objective of business is profit maximization. Profit maximization is not, to be sure, the objective of religious morality or of philosophical and legal ethics.

As the objective of business, it would be wrong to confuse profit maximization with the more familiar usage of these same words in the context of maximizing bottom-line (accounting) profits. Within profit maximization, and its emphasis on opportunity costs, ethics are assumed and implied. They are a substantial and necessary implication, inherent to the definition and practice of profit maximization.

Because opportunity costs are not included in the accounting formula for maximizing bottom-line profits, neither are the ethical considerations or imperatives they represent. Accounting incorporates only fixed and variable costs. Consequently, lacking an implied or inherent ethics, this understanding of "maximizing profits" (as opposed to *profit maximization*) requires and invites ethical principles from the outside, i.e., from philosophy, religion, and law.

But, to concentrate simply on bottom-line accounting profits is neither in the best interest of business or its mandate to pursue profit maximization. Its focus is too narrow and myopic, and results in an exaggerated emphasis on profits as ends in themselves.

IV

Individual

Ethics

and

Business

Ethics

For our purposes, however, we must distinguish business ethics from individual ethics. Our model of profit maximization creates and establishes a common perspective or common focus for ethical decision-making in business. We cannot expect a similar commonality to arise from the philosophical, legal, or religious ethics of individuals. There are simply too many differences to consider, and too many individual beliefs to counteract efficient decision making.

The biggest problem for business ethics is that individuals do not know their own ethics.

An analogy will help to explain our distinction between individual ethics and business ethics. Each and everyone of us is influenced, either directly or indirectly, by philosophical, legal, or religious interests. These influences may direct us towards one profession or another, towards choosing one kind of recreational activity or another. One may be influenced to choose to play football.

Once that choice is made, the rules of that particular game dominate any other individual beliefs or practices. The game could not be played otherwise. Imagine a game of football in which each person played according to his or her own rules of the game. Absolute anarchy and chaos would ensue.

In effect, once the choice has been made to enter into the game as a committed player, one's individual ethics would have to be bracketed or suspended, at least during the duration of the game.

Of course, one could choose not to play and base that decision on philosophical, legal, or religious beliefs. But, once the choice has been made to play football, the rules of football become first and foremost.

On a more practical note, how does one respond to a situation where there is a conflict between the personal ethics of the manager and the ethical considerations of a business decision? Suppose the senior management representative, on a committee of managers considering a potential business decision, must approve or disapprove the recommendations of the group. All of the fixed and variable costs have been calculated, the opportunity costs (including the ethical considerations) have been examined, and the consensus of the group is to proceed. However, the senior manager cannot reconcile his or her own personal ethics with the consensus. What does the profit-maximizing model require?

Profit maximization does not include personal ethics, only the opportunity costs of not being sensitive to the ethics of the community. However, it does include the inefficiencies that can be created by the manager if this conflict leads to paralysis or ineffectiveness. The manager has no recourse but to resign.

When Holiday Inn decided to open up a hotel and casino in Las Vegas, the president of the company faced a dilemma. His personal ethics were at odds with that of the community's acceptance of gambling. He knew the decision was in the best interest of the company, but he could not reconcile it with his own aversion to gambling, so he resigned.

To have given up all of the economic advantages and prestige of being president of a major corporation indicate the depth of commitment this man had to his personal ethics as well as to the profit-maximizing objectives of the company. His behavior was consistent with profit maximization.

Individual Ethics Versus Business Ethics

If, on the other hand, managers are able to reconcile conflicts between their personal ethics and those involved in any profit maximizing decision, there is no problem. They will continue to be effective, and their behavior will be consistent with the demands of profit maximization. However, anytime this happens, the manager has essentially changed his or her ethics because, *a priori*, one cannot enter into a process of reconciliation without changing one's values. From an economic perspective, it could be argued that the individual manager sold all or part of his or her ethics for another set of ethics.

One of the major postulates of economics is that personal attributes and talents, such as self respect, decency, and ethics are also economic goods, as are food, shelter, and health care. Like all economic goods, they are also bought and sold. Usually, the practice of buying and selling involves a money price. Sometimes, though, economic goods are bought and sold for other economic goods, i.e., bartering.

Like other people, managers barter with their ethics. They trade, as everyone does, their childhood ethics for adult ethics. If they didn't they wouldn't mature. They also sell their ethics for a money price, even putting aside or reconciling their personal ethics for a good-paying job.

Whether the behavior of buying and selling one's personal ethics is right or wrong is a question for the philosophical or religious moralist. We know that people do it, and the discipline of economics describes how they do it. However, we also know that the paradigm of profit maximization refers to personal ethics only to the extent that any conflict between the personal ethics of the manager and the ethics of the company which leads to inefficiencies requires that he or she resign.

V

A
Technical
Perspective

We have described the ethical implications of profit maximization from a behavioral perspective. These ethical implications can also be described from a more technical, mathematical perspective.

Technically, profit maximization is defined as that set of conditions where the marginal revenue of the firm is equal to its marginal cost (MR=MC) and the marginal cost curve must intersect the marginal revenue curve from below. For the manager of a firm, these conditions mean that the firm will continue to produce as long as the revenues from each unit sold exceed the cost. As more units are produced, the scarce resources used reach diminishing returns thereby causing marginal costs to increase. Eventually marginal cost will equal marginal revenue.

At that point, and only at that point, the firm will be operating at a level of output that guarantees the community the maximum amount of goods and services the firm can produce with the given set of resources it has.

If the firm produces at a point where marginal revenue is greater than marginal cost (MR>MC), it is choosing a level of output that is less than the profit maximizing output, and the community will have fewer goods and services.

Inasmuch as more homes, more education, more health care, etc. from a given set of resources are good, and less of these goods and services from a given set of resources is bad, there is an ethical dimension associated with any decision to produce at an output level where marginal revenue is greater than marginal cost.

A Technical Perspective

If the firm produces at a point where marginal revenue is less than marginal cost (MR<MC), it is choosing a level of output that is greater than the profit maximizing output, and the community has more goods and services. The problem with this decision is that it cost more to make these additional units of output than the revenues they generate, and the company will lose money.

It is axiomatic that any firm continuing to produce at a loss will eventually go out of business. So, what first appears to be a windfall for the community turns into a disaster. The firm shuts down, all of the things it once produced, including the windfall, disappear and the community has fewer goods and services.

There is an ethical dimension associated with the decision to produce where marginal revenue is less than marginal cost. Everyone would be hurt: managers, employees, stockholders, consumers--the greater community in which the business is located, the world community, i.e., all stakeholders.

A Technical Perspective

Since more is better than less from a given set of scarce resources, producing where marginal revenue is equal to marginal cost (MR=MC), profit maximizing, is efficient and ethical.

Producing where marginal revenue is greater than or less than marginal cost, not profit maximizing, is inefficient and unethical.

The ethical judgment rests first and foremost within practical economics and has consequences for individuals as well as for society as a whole.

Businesses know they are producing the right kind of goods and services because there is a demand for them. Businesses know they are producing the right amount of goods and services because they are producing at that level of output where marginal revenue is equal to marginal cost (MR=MC).

Producing at the lowest possible cost is probably the most recognizable tenet of business behavior. Failure to be cost-reduction sensitive could jeopardize the ability of the firm to survive. Business people are aware that lower costs give them a competitive advantage in the market place.

A Technical Perspective

Profit (π) = Total Revenue (TR) - Total Cost (TC)

$$\pi = TR - TC = f(x) = g(x)$$

The first-order conditions for profit maximization are:

$$d\pi \,/\, dx = f'(x) - g'(x) = O$$

Or

$$f'(x) = g'(x)$$

That is,

$$MR = MC$$

The second-order conditions must show:

$$d(d)(\pi) \,/\, d(x)(x) \,<\, 0$$

VI

Back
To
Basics

Efficiencies are usually calculated mathematically, and rarely translated into behavioral expectations. Our discussion moves from the more abstract mathematics to the more practical behavior, and concentrates on the ethical implications of both.

Although the science or discipline of economics originated in practical behavior, it developed into progressively more sophisticated and complex representations of that behavior in mathematical formulae. Now, when students study economics, they tend to focus on the mathematical representations rather than on the behavior they symbolize. Our objective is neither to criticize or interrupt this evolution, but to describe the behavior imaged in the numbers, graphs, and tables of economic text books, and to analyze that behavior in reference to its inherent ethical principles.

As we saw earlier, MR=MC can be translated into *producing the right kind and the right amount of goods and services consumers want at the lowest possible cost.* The right kind and the right amount of goods and services are determined by the market, that is, by supply and demand. Producing at the lowest possible cost is probably the most recognizable tenet of business behavior. Assuming consumer sovereignty (consumer wants) and low-cost market advantage (lowest possible cost), the behavior of profit maximization also recognizes that all resources used in production are scarce.

Accordingly, inefficient use of any scarce resource is unethical because it yields fewer goods and services to the community of individual consumers. Efficient use of scarce resources is ethical because it yields more goods and services to the community of consumers.

Within profit maximization, economic efficiencies are tied to cost-allocation decisions. These costs are usually defined as fixed, variable, and opportunity costs. In accounting, these cost-allocation decisions are defined simply in terms of fixed and variable costs. From this perspective, efficiency is focused on the allocation of fixed and variable costs alone. In economics, efficiency is a concern attached to opportunity costs in addition to fixed and variable costs. This difference is crucial because it moves the discussion from concern with the costs themselves to the manner in which they are incurred, and to the ethics involved in that process.

Opportunity costs are foregone goods and services that could have been produced from a given set of resources that were used to produce other goods and services. Once resources are allocated to establishing a used-car lot in an Amish community, or to producing chairs rather than automobiles, these resources are foregone. They can never be used to provide other goods and services for the community.

An automobile dealership in an Amish community would be a foolish undertaking. It would also be unethical, because it reflects a misappropriation and misuse of scarce resources. The realization that it would be offensive to Amish religious sensibilities is not, in itself, the basis of the unethical judgment, at least not for business. It is, to be sure, a concern which enters into opportunity-cost decision-making. However, the basis for that unethical judgment is the inefficient use of scarce economic resources. These same resources could have been used for another project which would not only have provided goods and services to consumers who want them, but which would also have been beneficial and profitable for all of the stakeholders.

Rather than focusing allocation decisions simply on fixed and variable costs, economic efficiency and profit maximization would situate the allocation of these costs within the wider context of opportunity costs. Internally, the focus would be on efficient use of the factors of production:

capital,

labor-time,

land,

creativity/ entrepreneurship.

The costs associated with the factors of production are described as payments: the payment to capitol is *interest*; to labor-time, *wages*; to land, *rent*; to creativity/entrepreneurship, *profits*. When each of the factors of production is regarded as a scarce resource, it is a matter of economic efficiency and of good ethics to pay each according to market standards, that is, the value of its marginal product. To pay either more or less is economically inefficient and unethical. It would also result in opportunity costs for the company. Paid less than the value of his/her marginal product, the employee, a scarce human resource, would leave the company. Paid more, the company's opportunity costs would result in fewer resources from which to produce the goods and services the community wants.

Externally, a firm's opportunity costs are tied to every consideration arising from the greater community in which the firm exists--from the immediacy of geographical location to philosophical, religious, legal, sociological, and cultural implications of the greater world. To choose to establish a used-car lot in an Amish community would be inefficient and unethical because the religious practices of a certain people within a certain place would not have been assessed or evaluated economically. Likewise, to ignore gift-exchanging in Japan would be inefficient and unethical.

From an ethical perspective, profit maximization and the efficiencies of profit maximization become the primary standard of judgment. Other implications, for example, legal, religious, philosophical, enter into the discussion as opportunity-cost considerations.

These considerations can and do change. The changing medical and political sentiment against smoking cigarettes would be an opportunity-cost consideration for the tobacco industry. Similarly, we're aware of changing pendulum swings, for example in the acceptance or prohibition of alcoholic beverages. Profit maximization and economic efficiency, valuing the sovereignty of the individual consumer and of the individual producer, reserve judgment, in the final analysis, to the market. However, it brings all of these market interests into the equation through long-term opportunity-cost considerations.

Opportunity-cost decision-making does not ignore conflict of interests between individual ethics and corporate ethics. Rather, it assumes a distinction between an individual's ethics and a company's ethics. As the individual's ethics could be religiously or philosophically determined, the company's ethics would be economically determined. It is, therefore, of tremendous importance that the individual defines his/her own ethics and that the company does the same. The individual is, then, in a position to judge whether to enter into, and contribute to, a certain industry or company. The ethical mandate of the company is to profit maximize through economic efficiencies. Ethical concerns about the company's product (the right kind of goods and services) are determined primarily by the market and by individual producers and consumers.

Earlier, we described the difference between individual ethics and corporate ethics through a football analogy. There are many reasons why an individual would want to play football, and these could be philosophical, psychological, or sociological in origin. There are also reasons why an individual would consider football unethical, e.g., a religious commitment to pacifism. However, once the individual decides to enter into the game, he or she plays by the rules of the game rather than by his or her individual rules of conduct.

This profit maximization paradigm for business ethics defines and sets the parameters for the rules of the game of business. To do so it focuses on economic efficiency measured by opportunity costs. It is grounded in business theory and practice, uses the language of business, and relates directly to the ordinary behavior of men and women in business. It has its own principles and assumptions. Foremost among these is economic efficiency through profit maximization.

This paradigm for business ethics also focuses on the generation of profit as indispensable for business and business ethics. It does so by distinguishing (economic) profit maximization from (accounting) maximizing profits. By enlisting its own economic principles and practices, it eliminates the need to turn to philosophy, religion, or law for ethical principles.

By focusing on opportunity costs and economic efficiency, this paradigm of profit maximization also provides a basis for arguing against any kind of self-aggrandizing greed at the expense of others. It seeks the personal and social well being of all stakeholders, and demands consideration of economic resources, people as well as things, as finite, scarce, and limited. This is a basic tenet to which religious, philosophical, and legal ethics can ascribe.

Perhaps more than anywhere else, this communal, social interdependence is reflected in a theoretical and practical attention to the costs and payments to each of the factors of production according to the respective contribution of each to profit.

Afterword

What we have tried to demonstrate is that the behavior of profit maximization includes an examination of the opportunity costs associated with all business decisions, and that ethical considerations represent some, although not all, of the opportunity costs of a given decision. We have also shown how our behavioral paradigm of profit maximization provides an objective basis for business ethics, i.e., a basis for business ethics which is inherent to business itself.

Profit maximization discourages flagrant disregard for community standards of pollution, safety, exploitation of human and natural resources, etc. Profit maximization demands that the *ethos* and *mores* of the community become integral to the decision-making process. In fact, issues raised by philosophical, religious, and legal concerns are also the concerns of business and its required sensitivity to the community as embodied in opportunity costs.

As we mentioned earlier, men and women in business make mistakes in their evaluation of these issues. But, so do lawyers, college professors, physicians, and ministers as they relate to their own professional ethics. We all know that there are business men and women who abuse the ethics of business. But, so do other professional men and women. That does not mean that profit maximization is invalid. What it means is that people who deliberately violate the precepts of this economic behavior are out of order.

As it relates to personal ethics, profit maximization is clear. It does not include them in the model. However, it does recognize the inefficiencies that can be generated in the event of a conflict between personal ethics and corporate ethics.

Selected Bibliography

Stieber, John and Primeaux, Patrick, "Economic Efficiency: A Paradigm for Business Ethics," *The Journal of Business Ethics,* 10,5: 335-339, 1991.

Stieber, John, "The Behavior of the NCAA: A Question of Ethics," *The Journal of Business Ethics*, 10,6: 445-449, 1991.

Primeaux, Patrick, "Experiential Ethics: A Blueprint for Personal and Corporate Ethics," *The Journal of Business Ethics*, 11,10: 779-788, 1992.

Primeaux, Patrick and Stieber, John, "Profit Maximization: The Ethical Mandate of Business," *The Journal of Business Ethics*, 13,4: 287-294, 1994.

Glossary

Profit Maximization:
   technical definition: The set of conditions where marginal revenue is equal to marginal cost (MR=MC), and where the marginal cost curve intersects the marginal revenue curve from below.
   behavioral definition: Producing the right kind and the right amount of goods and services the consumer wants at the lowest possible cost.

Economic Efficiency:
   The best use of scarce resources (factors of production) within the production process to avoid waste and abuse.

Factors of Production:
   Scarce economic resources which enter into production: Land, Labor-time, Capital, Creativity /entrepreneurship.

Payments to the Factors of Production:
   The costs of scarce resources which enter into production:Payment to land is rent; payment to labor-time is wages; payment to capital is interest; payment to creativity/entrepreneurship is profit.

Opportunity Costs:
   The foregone goods and services that could have been produced from a given set of resources which were used to produce some other goods and services, e.g.,the costs of the next best alternative with respect to payments to the factors of production. This is the basis for ethical decision-making in business, for it includes consideration of social and communal costs as well as dollars.

About the Authors

Pat Primeaux belongs to the Marists, an international congregation of Catholic priests and brothers. A native of Maurice, Louisiana, he was ordained in 1977 and awarded a Ph.D. in Theology by The University of Saint Michael's College, Toronto, in 1979. He taught graduate-level theology at Notre Dame Seminary in New Orleans, and part-time undergraduate religious studies at Loyola University of the South, also in New Orleans. He served as campus minister at Cleveland State University and as pastor of Sacred Heart Church in Gramercy, Louisiana. In 1989, he completed studies for an M.B.A. at the Edwin L. Cox School of Business, Southern Methodist University, Dallas, where he was an adjunct professor teaching a graduate course in business ethics with John Stieber.

At the present time, he teaches Moral Theology in the Marketplace, a course required of all undergraduate business majors, in the Department of Theology and Religious Studies, St. John's University, New York.

His first book, *Richard R. Niebuhr on Christ and Religion*, was published in 1981. His research and writing in the area of business ethics has been published in the *Journal of Business Ethics*. His work in the area of pastoral management has been published in *The Priest, Church, The New Theology Review,* and *The Journal of Ministry, Marketing & Management.*

John Stieber is Professor of Finance and Economics at the Edwin L. Cox School of Business, Southern Methodist University, Dallas, where he has taught courses in business ethics on both the undergraduate and graduate levels.

He has published in *The Journal of Business Ethics, The Journal of Business Strategy, The Virginia Medical Journal,* and *The Atlantic Economic Review.* He has also had feature articles in *USA Today, The Dallas Morning News, Texas Medicine,* and *Ethics.*

He is on the Board of Directors of Westech International, Jones-Blair Company, Inc., and Founder and Chairman of American Receivable Corporation. He has consulted for IBM, Frito Lay, NCR, the Belo Corporation, Baylor Hospital Center, and the University of Texas Health and Science Center, Dallas.

A legendary figure on the campus of Southern Methodist University, his graduate course in economics is frequently referred to as "Stiebernomics." In 1989, he was singled out as an outstanding professor by his students in *BusinessWeek's* annual survey of business schools. He has received several awards for his teaching as well as for his continuing dedication to the Edwin L. Cox School of Business.

Together, Primeaux and Stieber have collaborated on several articles for The *Journal of Business Ethics,* and have contributed a feature article to the forthcoming Blackwell's *Dictionary of Business Ethics.*

Index